MARKETING SECRETS

A SIMPLE
AND
EFFECTIVE
APPROACH

Khatryna W. House

Table Of Content

INTRODUCTION

What Is This Book All About?

As the North Star of entrepreneurship, marketing has a special place in the wide ocean of business tactics. It is the beacon of light that has catapulted new ventures into the stratosphere, revitalized aging behemoths, and made obscure concepts into international sensations. But depending on how it's used, marketing can either shine brightly or flicker softly, just like any other beacon.

Permit me to take you on a journey as we examine the amazing metamorphosis of visionary businesswoman Kathryn W. House. She began like many others, full of energy with a product that was going to change the game. She made a brilliant creation, but her path was not without confusion and disappointment. Her story serves as a living example of the incredible potential that can be found on a single piece of paper, or a one-page marketing strategy.

When Kathryn first started her entrepreneurial journey, her goals were unbounded. Equipped with a cutting-edge environmentally friendly household cleaner, she imagined a world where simplicity and sustainability coexisted. Her invention, "GreenGlow," had the power to completely change the way we clean our houses. It was safe for the environment, non-toxic, and extremely effective.

Still, there remained an issue. Like many business owners, Kathryn became disoriented in the maze of marketing options. She experimented with everything, including influencer collaborations, email newsletters, social media campaigns, and conventional print advertising. However, despite her best efforts, the outcomes were mediocre at best. The market was so full of options that the bright GreenGlow got lost in the din.

She was perplexed and frustrated one evening as she sat among a mound of marketing leaflets when Emily, an old friend, paid her an unexpected visit. As an experienced marketer herself, Emily was shocked by the disarray that had resulted from Kathryn's marketing initiatives. After glancing at the disorganized

documents, confusing advertisements, and conflicting messaging, she concluded that something needed to change.

During a hot cup of tea, Emily presented Kathryn with the idea of a one-page marketing plan, which would completely change her company. She imparted to Kathryn the straightforward yet effective notion that consistency, clarity, and concentration were essential for successful marketing. They set off on a path of strategic simplicity together.

They reduced GreenGlow to a single sheet of paper after hours of intensive concentration and brainstorming. Kathryn started using this one-page marketing plan as her guide. It outlined her target market, USP, and the methods through which she planned to connect with her clientele. It was more than simply a road plan; it was a daily reminder of what was really important for her marketing endeavors.

The outcome was just astounding. Kathryn carried out her marketing strategy with exactitude. She was perfectly aware of where to focus her time, energy, and resources. GreenGlow's message became very apparent, and customers reacted enthusiastically. The jumble of disparate marketing tactics became a purposeful symphony.

As the months went by, GreenGlow reached previously unheard-of heights. Its market share increased, and word of Kathryn's eco-friendly product caught on like wildfire. With the help of a one-page marketing plan, Kathryn W. House, who had previously been lost and struggling in the ocean, was able to find her way to success.

MARKETING

Imagine a world where products and ideas are born in obscurity, struggling to find their place in the vast marketplace. In this world, creativity remains uncelebrated, innovation languishes in the shadows, and exceptional solutions never see the light of day. It's a world where your brilliance remains hidden, your story untold, and your potential unrealized.

Now, let's step into a different world—a world where your ideas become irresistible, where your brand emerges as a beacon of desire, and where your message resonates with the hearts and minds of your audience. In this world, marketing is the wand that transforms obscurity into prominence, where the mundane becomes memorable, and where businesses, both big and small, can shape destinies.

This book is your ticket to that world, a world where marketing is the magical force that turns ordinary products into extraordinary sensations and transforms budding entrepreneurs into household names. Here, we embark on an exciting journey through the ever-evolving landscape of marketing, where creativity meets strategy, data informs decision-making, and innovation knows no bounds.

In the pages that follow, we will unravel the secrets of successful marketing. We'll explore how the world's most iconic brands have seduced their audiences, how data-driven insights have revolutionized the marketing game, and how you can harness the very essence of what makes your brand unique.

Whether you're an established marketing maven seeking fresh perspectives or a newcomer eager to discover the enchantment of marketing, this book is your guide. We'll dive deep into the art and science of marketing, from understanding the psychology of consumer behavior to mastering the digital realm, all while keeping an eye on the ever-changing trends that redefine the industry.

Marketing isn't just a department or a job title; it's a superpower that can catapult your ideas into the hearts and wallets of your target audience. It's the magic wand that transforms obscurity into stardom, and it's a realm where innovation meets storytelling to create unforgettable experiences.

So, are you ready to uncover the secrets of marketing magic? Let's turn the page and embark on this thrilling adventure through the world of marketing, where the possibilities are as endless as your imagination.

We will explore the art and science of writing your own marketing Secret in great detail in this book. We'll analyze the business triumphs of individuals like Kathryn, delve into the psychology of consumer behavior, and uncover the tactics that transform an idea into a tangible product. So grab your seatbelts, reader, and get ready for an incredible adventure into the realm of marketing, where clarity is the light that guides you from chaos to success and simplicity is king. Greetings and welcome to the world of marketing secret

Chapter 1

Selecting Your Target Market

Your objective market establishes the vibe for your whole advertising system — from how you create and name your items or administrations directly through to the showcasing channels you use to advance them.

Here is a clue before we dive in: Your objective market isn't "everybody" (except if you're Google). Your errand in characterizing your objective market is to recognize and figure out a more modest, pertinent specialty so you can rule it. Everything revolves around limiting your concentration while extending your compass.

In this aide, we'll assist you with realizing who's now cooperating with your business and your rivals, then, at that point, utilize that data to foster an unmistakable objective market   as   you   construct   your   image

What is a target market?

An objective market is the particular gathering you need to reach with your marketing message. They are individuals who are probably going to purchase your items or administrations, and they are joined by a few normal qualities, similar to socioeconomics and ways of behaving.

The more plainly you characterize your objective market, the better you can figure out how and where to arrive at your optimal possible clients. You can begin with general classifications like twenty to thirty year olds or single parents, yet you really want to get substantially more nitty gritty than that to accomplish the most ideal transformation rates.

Go ahead and get profoundly unambiguous. This is tied in with focusing on your promoting endeavors really, not preventing individuals from purchasing your item.

Individuals who are excluded from your designated showcasing can in any case purchase from you — they're simply not your top center while creating your advertising system. You can't target everybody, except you can offer to everybody.

Your objective market ought to be founded on research, not a hunch. You really want to pursue individuals who truly need to purchase from you, regardless of whether they're not the clients you initially set off to reach.

What is target market segmentation?

Target market segmentation is the method involved with partitioning your objective market into more modest, more unambiguous gatherings. It permits you to make a more pertinent showcasing message for each gathering.

Recall — you can't be everything to all individuals. However, you can be various things to various gatherings.

For instance, as a veggie lover, I've eaten a lot of Unthinkable Burgers. I'm certainly an objective client. However, vegans are a shockingly little objective market section for Unimaginable Food sources: just 10% of their client base.

That is the reason Inconceivable Food varieties' most memorable public promoting effort was certainly not designated at me:

How to define your target market

Step 1. Gather information on your ongoing clients

An extraordinary initial phase in sorting out who most needs to purchase from you is to distinguish who is now utilizing your items or administrations. When you comprehend the main qualities of your current client base, you can pursue more individuals like that.

Contingent upon how somebody interfaces with your business, you could have just a little data about them, or a great deal. This doesn't mean you ought to add a great deal of inquiries to your request or select in process only for crowd research purposes — this can pester clients and result in deserted shopping baskets.

Yet, do make certain to utilize the data you normally gain to figure out patterns and midpoints.

Your CRM is a goldmine here. UTM boundaries joined with Google Investigation can likewise give valuable data about your clients.

A few information focuses you should consider are:

Age: You don't have to get excessively unambiguous here. It won't probably have an effect whether your typical client is 24 or 27. Be that as it may, knowing which ten years of life your clients are in can be extremely helpful.

Area (and time region): Where on earth do your current clients reside? As well as understanding which geographic regions to focus on, this assists you with sorting out what hours are generally significant for your client care and agents to be on the

web, and what time you ought to plan your social promotions and presents to guarantee best perceivability.

Language: Don't expect your clients to communicate in a similar language you do. Also, don't expect them to communicate in the predominant language of their (or your) current actual area.

Spending influence and examples: How much cash do your ongoing clients need to spend? How would they move toward buys in your cost class?

Interests: What do your clients get a kick out of the chance to do, other than utilizing your items or administrations? What Programs do they watch? What different organizations do they connect with?

Challenges: What trouble spots are your clients confronting? Do you comprehend how your item or administration assists them with tending to those difficulties?

Phase of life: Are your clients liable to be understudies? Inexperienced parents? Guardians of youngsters? Retired people?

On the off chance that you're selling B2B items, your classifications will look somewhat changed. You should gather data about the size of organizations that purchase from you, and data about the titles of individuals who will generally settle on the purchasing choices. Is it true or not that you are showcasing to the Chief? The CTO? The social promoting director?

Step 2: Incorporate social information
Virtual entertainment examination can be an incredible approach to finishing up the image of your objective market. They assist you with figuring out who's collaborating with your social records, regardless of whether those individuals are not yet clients.

These individuals are keen on your image. Social investigation can give a ton of data that could be useful to you to grasp the reason why. You'll likewise find out about potential market sections you might not have remembered to focus on previously.

You can likewise utilize social standing by listening to assist with distinguishing individuals who are discussing you and your item via online entertainment, regardless of whether they follow you.

If you have any desire to arrive at your objective market with social advertisements, carbon copy crowds are a simple method for contacting more individuals who share qualities with your best clients.

Step 3. Look at the Competition

Since it has become so obvious who's as of now connecting with your business and purchasing your items or administrations, now is the right time to see who's drawing in with the opposition.

Understanding what your rivals are doing can assist you with responding to a few key inquiries:

> ➢ Are your rivals pursuing a similar objective market portion as you are?
> ➢ Is it true that they are arriving at portions you hadn't remembered to consider?
> ➢ How can they situate themselves?

Our aide on the most proficient method to do contender research via virtual entertainment strolls you through the most ideal ways to utilize social apparatuses to assemble contender bits of knowledge.

You will not have the option to get point by point crowd data about individuals collaborating with your rivals, however you'll have the option to get a general feeling of the methodology they're taking and whether it's permitting them to make a commitment on the web.

This examination will assist you with understanding which market contenders are focusing on and whether their endeavors seem, by all accounts, to be powerful for those sections.

Step 4: Clarify the worth of your product or administration

This boils down to the key differentiation all advertisers should comprehend among elements and advantages. You can list the highlights of your item the entire day, yet nobody will be persuaded to purchase from you except if you can make sense of the advantages.

Your item is or does highlight. The advantages are the outcomes. How does your item make somebody's life simpler, or better, or seriously fascinating?

In the event that you don't as of now have a reasonable rundown of the advantages of your item, now is the ideal time to begin conceptualizing now. As you make your advantage proclamations, you'll likewise as a matter of course be expressing some essential data about your interest group.

For instance, assuming your administration assists individuals with tracking down somebody to take care of their pets while they're away, you can be quite certain that your market will have two fundamental fragments:)

1. animal people
2. existing or expected pet-sitters.

On the off chance that you don't know precisely the way in which clients benefit from utilizing your items, why not ask them in a review, or even a web-based entertainment survey?

You could find that individuals utilize your items or administrations for purposes you haven't even considered. That may, thus, change how you see your objective market for future deals.

Step 5: Create a Target Market Statement
Presently it is the ideal time to bubble all that you've found such a long way into one basic proclamation that characterizes your objective market. This is really the most vital phase in making a brand situating explanation, however that is an undertaking for one more day. For the time being, we should adhere to making an explanation that plainly characterizes your objective market.

For instance, here's Zipcar's image situating explanation, as referred to in the exemplary promoting text Kellogg on Advertising. We're keen on the initial segment of the assertion, which characterizes the objective market:

"To metropolitan dwelling, instructed, techno-sharp buyers who stress over the climate that people in the future will acquire, Zipcar is the vehicle sharing help that allows you to set aside cash and decrease your carbon impression, causing you to feel you've made a savvy, capable decision that shows your obligation to safeguarding the climate."

Zipcar isn't focusing on all occupants of a specific city. They're not in any event, focusing on every one individual in a given city who doesn't claim a vehicle. They're explicitly focusing on individuals who:

➢ live in a metropolitan region
➢ have a specific level of instruction
➢ are alright with innovation
➢ are worried about the climate

These are interests and ways of behaving that Zipcar can explicitly target utilizing social substance and social advertisements.

They additionally help to direct the organization's general way to deal with its administration, as confirmed by the remainder of the situating proclamation.

While making your objective market proclamation, attempt to integrate the main segment and conduct qualities you've recognized. For instance:

Our objective market is [gender(s)] matured [age range], who live in [place or kind of place], and like to [activity].

Try not to feel like you really want to adhere to these specific identifiers. Perhaps orientation is unessential for your market, yet you have three or four critical ways of behaving to consolidate in your explanation.

In the event that you offer numerous items or administrations, you could have to make an objective market proclamation for each market portion. For this situation, characterizing purchaser personas is valuable.

Target market examples

1. Nike target market

In spite of its ongoing business sector mastery, Nike really gives an extraordinary illustration of what can turn out badly when you attempt to target an excessively broad group of people.

Nike began as a running shoe organization. During the 1980s, they attempted to extend their objective market past sprinters to incorporate anybody who needed agreeable shoes. They sent off a line of easygoing shoes, and it tumbled.

Listen to this: Non-sprinters were at that point purchasing Nike shoes to stroll to work, or for other easygoing purposes. Nike detected this as a chance to grow. All things considered, they weakened their image guarantee, and the organization really began losing cash.

The illustration, as per organization pioneer Phil Knight?

"At last, we discovered that we believed that Nike should be the world's best games and wellness organization and the Nike brand to address sports and wellness exercises. When that's what you say, you have a center."

While Nike would unquestionably not prevent easygoing clients from purchasing its shoes, the organization pulled together everything from item improvement to showcasing on its objective market: competitors, everything being equal, from expert to brew association.

As a matter of fact, understanding the significance of the center drove Nike into a profoundly viable technique of target market division. The brand has different objective business sectors for its different product offerings.

On friendly terms, that implies they utilize various records to arrive at their different objective market gatherings. Nobody account attempts to be everything to all clients.

The post beneath Nike's overall Instagram account focuses on the portion of their crowd keen on design and way of life items.

Also, that implies … the brand has had the option to get back to promoting its items explicitly for easygoing wear. It simply arrives at the relaxed objective market through unexpected directions in comparison to what it utilizes for its athletic business sectors. It's an alternate objective market section, and an alternate promoting message

Like Nike, you could have one objective market, or many, contingent upon the size of your image. Recall that you can talk really to each target market fragment in turn.

2.Takasa target market

Takasa is a Canadian retail homewares organization that works in natural, fair exchange bedding and shower materials.

Here is their objective market as characterized by originators Ruby and Kuljit Rakhra: "Our objective market is the LOHAS portion, and that implies Family Ways of life of Wellbeing and Manageability. This gathering is as of now living, or endeavoring to carry on with, a green way of life … We realize our objective demo is extremely cognizant about what their families consume, as well as the effect this utilization has on the climate."

In their social substance, they obviously distinguish the item includes generally essential to their objective market: natural materials and fair work rehearses.

3. The City of Port Alberni's target market

For what reason does a city require an objective market? In Port Alberni's case, the city is attempting to "draw in venture, business valuable open doors and new occupants." With that in mind, they sent off a rebranding and promoting effort.

What's more, a showcasing effort, obviously, needs an objective market. This is the way the city characterized it:

"Our objective market is youngsters and youthful families 25 to 45 years old who are enterprising leaning, family arranged, gutsy, partake in a functioning way of life, want a potential chance to add to development, knowledgeable and talented experts or dealers." In their social substance, they feature sporting open doors focused on those dynamic and daring youthful families, in any event, utilizing the handle @PlayinPA.

4. White House Black Market target market

White House Underground market is a ladies' design image. On their website, they present their ideal client as follows:

"Our client … is solid yet inconspicuous, present day yet ageless, diligent yet nice."

That is a fine depiction while talking straightforwardly to clients. In any case, the promoting division needs an objective market definition with a couple of additional particulars. Here is the itemized target market as depicted by the organization's previous president:

"Women [with a middle age of approximately 45] who are in a stage of life when they are highly engaged and fundamentally a functioning woman make up our target market. She's likely got a couple of children left at home [or] … her kids might be out of the house and while heading to school."

With their hashtag #WHBMPowerhouse, they center around this vital segment of ladies in their 40s with occupied home residences and vocations

Two significant variables that influence the choice of the right objective market are

A) Engaging quality of a given market portion and how intently it guides to the business' goals, capacities, and assets within reach.

While assessing the engaging quality of a given market or market fragment, there are a couple of viewpoints you ought to consider.

Size of the market or market section. For instance, on the off chance that the market portion is the school going understudy's gathering, the market size in view of demography and geology, will be 20 million in the US.

The development pace of the market or market section. This gives perceivability to how rapidly your business needs are proportional to the development paces of the market so you don't lose the piece of the pie to different players. Generally converts into mindfulness missions and ads over a supported period.

Portion rivalry. A vital component that can't be trifled with. You must be on top of the abilities of the opposition and the procedures they are prepared to do, so you get to raise the stakes than them while perhaps not less, obviously, in light of your own business' capacities.

Brand dedication. Assuming you enter a market that is high on brand dependability, it will be a test to get new buyers snared on to your item, except if you have the trust in the uniqueness and capacity of your own item.

A gauge of an achievable piece of the pie given your own financial plan imperatives and how much the opposition can spend. Quarterly targets can be chosen to meet generally monetary targets.

Settle on what ought to be the expected piece of the pie to make back the initial investment on interest into the product offering.

Self-evaluation of your business' capacity in laying out a hold and getting a huge enough piece of the pie. A fair evaluation of your business' capacity will far in accomplishing achievement and long haul supportability.

Your ongoing responsibility and striving after extension will drive your edge assumptions. Be that as it may, the edge is likewise an element of cutthroat valuing, you ought to track down the slim line between the two for ideal increases. Devices used to acquire this information Statistical surveying and Examination envelopes.

B) How appropriate is the market fragment to the business' own drawn out targets and objectives.

The business ought to likewise investigate and comprehend on the off chance that the market or market portion being taken a gander at adjusts well to its own goals, capacities, and assets.

The business ought to evaluate if the item on offer adding prevalent worth or filling in a huge hole on the lookout.

Will the business and its items be adversely or emphatically affected by its introduction to the new market section.

The business should survey in the event that it will actually want to be deft and increase or down premise the interest and how well is their circulation channel prepared to take the new send off.

Capital speculation ought to be surveyed against the business' ongoing assets and liabilities.

Methodologies for Target Market Determination

While there are numerous techniques that can be applied to the choice of the objective market, here are probably the most widely recognized and instinctive ones.

Single-fragment: Every one of your assets on new item dispatches are centered around one market section, ordinarily upheld by an extremely nitty gritty and clear cut market portion. Private ventures with their restricted assets frequently pick this system.

Particular specialization: For this situation, different showcasing blends are served to various market portions, a numerous fragment methodology that showcases a similar item by means of various circulation channels and reasonable limited time messages for separate sections.

Item specialization: A solitary product offering specialization fitting it to different market fragments.

Market-specialization: The business could decide to serve the market portion with different item contributions covering different highlights that are a prerequisite in the market fragment.

Full-market inclusion: Something that organizations with firm capital sponsorship and well established in the business take to catch a large portion of the new market for the most part offering a separate promoting blend for various market fragments. Here and there a solitary undifferentiated promoting blend is proposed to all market fragments chosen.

Organizations ought to likewise direct an investigation of a few other significant elements prior to settling available or market sections they need to play in.

They ought to comprehend the way of life of the purchasers they are making the item for. This likewise somehow or another decides how faithful the buyers are to a brand or item. In the event that the items in the fragment despise an extraordinary brand following, the business ought to make important changes in the portion of assets in the activity of making a brand esteem.

The segment of the purchasers. Age, of the multitude of elements, is a key component that generally chooses the promoting system of the item. Businesses can't advertise similar items generally speaking to individuals of all age groups, they have various assumptions and necessities.

The pay of buyers and their spending power. Interrelated to the age factor, buyers in a specific age section will generally spend significantly more on specific items and brands than others. For instance, the school going gathering will be substantially more in style than the average workers.

Orientation is a main consideration in choosing the objective market or market portion. Organizations might decide to utilize a similar item with various advertisement crusades and special directives for various sexual orientations. For instance, take a washing cleanser. Presently there are various motivations behind why cleanser or washing cleanser requests to various individuals. We should list the most widely recognized.

Some utilize it for its unremarkable reason, to scrub down, however they additionally could connect it with the sensation of newness or the after-shower aroma. Decision of the brand could rely upon the sort of new scent a cleanser could possibly emit after a shower.

A few use it as insurance against microorganisms and contaminations. So the scent doesn't exactly make any difference and consequently the choice of getting cleanser from a store rack frequently spins around what is imprinted on the cleanser or what was advanced in a promotion crusade.
Some for decency and clear skin. Again the choice of a buyer to get the cleanser from the store rack relies upon whether the item depiction and its promotion crusade have demonstrated anything with this impact and how successfully it has done as such.

Summarily, target Market choice is a term that is generally related with new item improvement and dispatches. It is a significant phase of the item or administration send off as it hones the promoting technique adding to the outcome of the item or administration on the lookout. It includes assessing how rewarding different

sections in the commercial center are, and which portion will give the best return of ventures and time it takes to enter the market to a critical degree.
Target Market choice is an action that comes just after the business has fragmented its market, has proactively dissected the buyer, and separated them into general classes. At the market determination stage, the business needs to choose the most

rewarding business sector for better edges and long haul supportability in view of the size and development of a specific portion. Rivalry in the market can't be overlooked also. The progress of your item essentially really relies on how the given market is divided between contenders and whether you can break into their piece of the pie, and the methodologies the opposition will utilize to handle your new item in the commercial center.

CHAPTER 2

Reaching prospect with advertising media

Subsequent to having your statistical surveying and sharpening your message, you really want to spread the news about your business. Be that as it may, imagine a scenario in which you have a restricted spending plan.

Publicizing is one of the most misconstrued and costly pieces of the marketing system. Time again I address entrepreneurs who:

> ➢ Have no clue assuming their marketing really works
> ➢ Utilize one media to arrive at their interest group
> ➢ Physically handle supporting their possibilities

Does this seem like you? I'm not saying you're doing everything wrong. I simply figure you can head in a superior bearing in the event that you understand what great publicizing is and how to use the right media methodology.

Could you at any point accept Walt Disney confronted a similar quandary?

During the beginning of Mickey Mouse, Walt was frequently troubled with obligation and needed to track down inventive ways of publicizing what he was doing.

During the 1920s, when most head honchos disregarded sound movies as a craze, the generally obscure Walt Disney saw an open door. He conceded to delivering the principal completely synchronized sound animation. Walt integrated innovation to match up the sound to the movement, and circulated the third of his Mickey Mouse kid's shows, Steamer Willie — the animation that would make the mouse famous.

Being that Walt was a visionary, history rehashed the same thing in the 50's when Walt grasped the force of a previously unheard-of medium: TV. He embraced it as a method for giving diversion to the general population and money for his plan to fabricate amusement parks.

The greater part a century after the fact, the Walt Disney Organization keeps on conveying top of the line diversion in their amusement parks and with solid brands like the Disney Station, ABC, ESPN, Wonder, and Lucasfilm.

Just like Walt Disney

Publicizing media is the vehicle you'll use to convey your message to your objective market and very much like Walt did, you want to painstakingly choose and oversee it to guarantee the best profit from your speculation (return for money invested). No matter what the media you pick — radio, television, print, online entertainment, Website optimization, content, or email — you want to grasp the quirks of each.

Measure the success of your Marketing Campaign

Recall that what gets estimated gets made due. This is the way you can gauge your missions:

Did the promoting battle get you more cash-flow than it set you back?

What was the profit from speculation (return on initial capital investment) of that mission?

On the off chance that the expense is greater than the income, think of it as a disappointment. In the event that it's costing you not exactly the benefits it's getting, it's a triumph.

Rather than attempting to "get your name out there," focus on getting the name of your possibilities to your business

Mass promoting is, as such, a mission zeroed in on getting your name out there, on telling individuals you exist and trusting somebody's answers. This sort of advertising is best passed on to huge organizations with large enough pockets to attempt to arrive at everybody. In the event that you're a little to medium business you ought not be attempting this technique. All things considered, get to know your clients and target them.

A genuine model on how you can keep a mission responsible

Take a vehicle wash, for instance. Web-based entertainment and internet promoting are two extraordinary ways of publicizing this sort of business. The figures underneath are adjusted for effortlessness.

For each 10,000 web-based impressions that the mission gathers in a month, 1000 individuals answer, giving the vehicle wash a really good 10% reaction rate. Out of the thousand individuals who answered, 25 changed over into clients.

This technique permits the vehicle wash to ascertain its client securing cost. The 25 new clients that came about because of a mission with a complete expense of $300 makes their client procurement cost equivalent to $12.

Client procurement and the lifetime worth of a client, joined with the best media for your message, are three of the main parts for your promoting responsibility and viability.

Returning to our vehicle wash model, on the off chance that the item or administration this business offers to its clients made them under $12 all through the client's lifetime esteem, this was a terrible mission (negative return for money invested).

Normally, you can get an essential vehicle wash for around $6 to $9, the cost frequently duplicates in the event that you need "the works." However, regardless of whether a first time client spends the $12 to make back the initial investment with the cost of their securing, the client could experience passionate feelings for the item and administration, and keep on purchasing from this business, totally changing the financial matters of the mission.

The typical driver washes their vehicle like clockwork. Assuming every vehicle wash is $7, the worth of this client each year is no less than $168, bringing $156 of only benefits to the business (positive return on initial capital investment). On the off chance that she washes her vehicle one time each week, Incomes leap to $336. Might you at any point envision the benefits in the event that you have a client forever?

Most Common Digital Media

Digital media offers a clear and efficient means of communicating your message while enabling laser-focused targeting. But the ability to track every aspect of your campaign is my favorite feature of the more recent digital media.. Here are five of the most common digital media where you can market your business and keep track of your investment:

Social Media

Social media allows you the opportunity to 'refine' your business; the opportunity to associate with individuals in an individual manner, an exceptionally useful asset for your promotion.

Exploit each choice out there and speak with individuals as a delegate, instead of a nondescript organization. Recall that by the day's end, all of us are individuals. Assuming that you customize your cooperations with your crowd, you'll obtain improved results.

Social Media Advertising

Many page proprietors feel that natural arrival in virtual Social media is sufficient to have an effect. This was valid during the main long periods of informal organizations, yet tragically that is not true anymore. Facebook and numerous other web-based entertainment networks have become pay-to-play.

Each web-based entertainment network is dealing with algorithmic feeds, important presents are displayed on the client in view of past ways of behaving and inclinations. Natural posts from your Facebook page will just arrive at a negligible portion of your supporters, and that number is dropping, as per Brian Boland, head of the Promotions Item Showcasing group at Facebook. (You can peruse the entire article here.)

Email Marketing

Email marketing is an amazing asset for gaining, drawing in, and holding clients to assist your business with flourishing. This is an immediate and individual method for drawing in with possibilities and clients, and with the expanded utilization of cell phones and cell phones, essentially everybody includes their email inside simple reach.

Powerful email advertising will assist you with expanding maintenance, commitment, and income for your business.

Buyers actually really like to get brand interchanges by means of email, as indicated by ongoing examination. Email is the most favored brand correspondence channel for respondents of the concentrate in all ages, from gen X-er to Age Z shoppers.

Content Marketing

This is a showcasing methodology zeroed in on giving significant, pertinent, and reliable substance to draw in and hold your market, at last expanding your benefits. You are giving genuinely significant and helpful substance to your possibilities and clients, making you a specialist in your industry. There are something like three primary reasons — and benefits — for organizations to utilize content advertising:

> ➤ Expansion in deals
> ➤ Decline in costs
> ➤ Higher client faithfulness

Google Adwords

Adwords permits your business to appear and be seen by planned clients at the exact instant that they're scanning on Google for the things you offer, helping you:

- ➤ Draw in additional clients
- ➤ Contact the perfect individuals brilliantly
- ➤ Publicize locally or worldwide
- ➤ Best thing: You just compensate for results, when your crowd answers.

One is the most hazardous number in marketing.

One is the most risky number in your business. You can't rely upon only one wellspring of leads, just a single significant provider, one client, one sort of item, one kind of media. A typical slip-up with regards to the media system is to have just a single wellspring of new business.

It's an extremely predicament to wind up in. A business that has a weak link is fragile and a little change in its conditions could make destroying impacts. See what befell the Demise Star in Star Wars: one little imperfection can cut everything down.

How To Reach Prospect Clients

Associations attract conceivable outcomes through advancing, which offers various possible opportunities to get innovative. The way to powerful prospecting is the consistent and dependable use of numerous exhibiting channels, pushing toward clients from different headings immediately. Business people who center around a couple of streets during the arrangements cycle gain the most headway.

Think about the going with strategies for attracting potential clients to your business:

Advance your site for your area. Your web exhibiting tries presumably to consolidate website improvement. Exactly when you improve your site for your local neighborhood, in your space track down you even more easily.

Make and keep an internet based amusement presence. Online amusement pages gather brand care and set out frameworks organization open entryways you would never have regardless had.

Show your industry ability. This somewhat long system for bargain prospecting integrates creating website web diaries, whitepapers, and various reports and taking action to talk at get-togethers and studios.

Network. If you would portray your framework's organization attempts as conflicting, consider achieving more. Putting together works, but given that you work it.

Be consistent. Like frameworks organization, conflicting promoting offers sporadic results. Be consistent in your promoting procedure to make the most of your undertakings.

Be direct. Conceivable outcomes would like to attract with clear associations than those with no humankind or character. Show your potential clients what your character is.

What Are the Methods for Pushing toward Conceivable outcomes?

Bargains prospecting incorporates advancing undertakings to push toward ideal clients. Outreach bunches do this in various ways, including:

Warm calls: Regardless of the way that we don't recommend random selling, warm calling can give splendid results. A warm call contrasts from a random sale since you have a remark, not something to sell. Follow up your warm calls with messages or directives for the best results.

Email displaying: Email is an unprecedented stage for B2C and B2B prospecting. Assemble email addresses, and get creative to make the most of your email advancing.

References: Use your ongoing business contacts to make reference to social events.

Content promoting: You can show up at conceivable outcomes indirectly through quality substance. Give critical and illuminating substance to develop your picture's power and attract qualified leads.

Instead of relying upon a lone technique, endeavor them all and see what ends up being brutal for your business.

The best strategy to Prospect Better

Viable arrangements prospecting strategies make a restricted arrangements pipe that goals qualified conceivable outcomes. Expecting your arrangements pipeline gives off an impression of being unnecessarily obstructed, making you miss bargains since you're too clamoring to sort out cold prospects, consider limiting your arrangements channel. For sure, you will get less leads by and large, yet the ones you truth be told do get will undoubtedly change over.

By focusing on the idea of leads rather than the sum, you can even more really spread out buyer personas and separate leads into groupings considering the best method for reaching each conceivable buyer.

Recognizing clear personas for your B2C and B2B buyers will help you with interacting less complex with drives, those prospects who need results like those you've accomplished for existing clients — direct arrangements trailblazers to these opportunities for extra changes.

7 Out of the Compartment Prospecting Considerations

Though a prospecting method routinely consolidates messages and warm calls, you can similarly benefit from contemplating the case. The best method for getting a couple of innovative contemplations is to get to know your potential outcomes. This endeavor used to require a lot of effort, yet you can learn about an arrangement prospect quickly by finding their online diversion profiles.

While getting to know an ensured probability through virtual diversion, look at individual information that will help you with talking with them effectively. Does this lead value entertaining pictures, or is their profile more serious? Do they share anything for all plans and reasons with you or a sales rep?

Right when you get to know who your potential outcomes are, you can interact with them on a human level and suggest tweaked deals with any consequences regarding their interests.

Consider the contemplations under to get creative with your prospecting attempts:

1. Creative Gifts To Transport off Conceivable outcomes

Business people and specialists typically send gifts to conceivable outcomes, yet the old checked mug or pen won't propel a ton nowadays. Conceivable outcomes answer better to altered gifts that say the agent brains with the eventual result of getting to know them.

Coming up next are two or three innovative gift contemplations for anticipated conceivable outcomes:

New toy: Sort out what your chance appreciates, and gift them another toy. Send the tech ace one more device or the cake expert one more book of recipes.

Region based gift: Use your chance's region to tweak a lot of liners or wall workmanship.

Valuable gift: Pick an establishment neighborhood to your chance and give in their name.

Take on program: Use "embrace a" tasks to send critical gifts. For example, association mascots make exceptional gathering gifts.

2. Inventive Approaches to getting Arrangements Game plans

Notwithstanding the way that you shouldn't stop sending those FedEx letters or messages, you could have better karma arranging bargain game plans using more innovative procedures. Settle on ways that superstar your fascinating person and make people laugh. Horseplay and entertaining people are significant, but attempt to ground the humor in what you're promoting.

The following are an occurrences of creative approaches to getting bargains plans:

Joke: Author and business visionary Trash Ambirge sold land advancement space by sending association roof shingles that read "You + Me = Arrangements through the housetop."

Senseless commitment: Resulting in getting no response to their standard mail, Redditor u/thesonofnarcs sent a goliath rich crocodile to Outback Steakhouse. They evidently returned immediately.

Significant video: Many free extensions exist for video illuminating, including Stage, Wistia, and Vidyard. Use one of these to make short, significant accounts. Make your chance a tune, play out a rap, or give your endeavor to take care of business while rearranging.

With respect to getting bargain game plans, it pays to stand out and lay out a drawn out association.Bargains Exertion Considerations.

Instead of relying upon crisp work to drive bargains, stay imaginative, and stand separated from the resistance. Two or three creative arrangements outreach considerations include:

Consider new ideas: Don't become involved with anything various arrangements specialists do. Taking everything into account, endeavor to stand out. For example, "ruler of arrangements" Jeffrey Gitomer doesn't give out business cards. In light of everything, he disseminates coins featuring his face, contact information, and a canny line, "In bargains we trust."

Do whatever it takes not to ignore competitors: Various business people and sales reps don't put forth reference to competitors during attempt calls, despite how this may be a mistake. You can use your adversaries to show how your thing or organization stands separated from the rest.

Do whatever it takes not to minimize guards: The receptionists, colleagues, and HR work force are people you talk with before the leads. These people probably won't have purchasing power, but they truly can influence a boss.

3. The best technique to Prospect On the web

Finding incredible conceivable outcomes requires the usage of various stages. Could we look at a couple of basic ones and how they work with bargains prospecting:

Email: Business visionaries and arrangements stars use prospecting messages to get their business message to qualified leads. Supporting an expected client through email offers various opportunities to keep prospects secured.

Social Media: Virtual diversion stages like Facebook and LinkedIn offer publicizing for convincing prospecting. If you don't have the monetary arrangement for paid social offering, use electronic diversion get-togethers to track down prospects on the web.

Web enhancement: You can use Web advancement procedures to drive assigned traffic to your website. Integrate worked on satisfaction for potential outcomes at each period of the buyer adventure.

PPC: Lead age is clear with assigned Pay Per Snap notices in light of the fact that these put your business on the top page of Google.

4. Inventive Approaches to getting Openness

A gigantic piece of arrangements prospecting incorporates getting your name out there to your ideal chance. Extraordinary openness drives more leads, whether your business is sparkling clean or numerous years old. Consider the going with prospecting ways of getting more noteworthy openness:

Give out free resources. People trust reliable subject matter experts, so don't swarm your industry authority. Share your exceptional pieces of information and what you've understood through your tutoring and experiences with your fundamental vested party.

Transform into a supporter. Do you incorporate a most cherished cause inside your industry? Transform into an advertiser for change and show your potential outcomes that you care about the destiny of your industry.

Volunteer your time. You can get exceptional openness from contributing your huge venture to the less fortunate. Take your effort gathering to a soup kitchen, raise money for a nearby crisis center, or find substitute approaches to contributing.

Produce media. Make a YouTube channel, a computerized recording, a public transmission, or another kind of media to help authority and openness.

5. Messages

Lead support incorporates sending messages.

What Makes Advertising Effective?

Let's get real here for a minute, most organizations need to get however much openness from the media as could reasonably be expected. It feels quite a bit better to be seen on bulletins, television plugs, in distributions, on the web, makes no difference either way.

Dmitry Dragilev compares this to lights over broadway. Be that as it may, indeed, your interest group is at home watching Netflix. So squandering your cash on media which your possibility never consumes is terrible for business and your financial balance.

It feels much better to have the option to say, "I've been highlighted in Forbes or The New York Times." However, that is simply taking care of your self image. You truly need to bring in cash in the shadows, and you do this through designated publicizing. This has worked for me.

So what makes advertising effective?

There's really no need to focus on getting your name out to a more extensive crowd. It's tied in with associating with the right crowd and inspiring them to settle on your item or administration. This implies having an extremely clear image of who your crowd is and what is most important to them. This blog tells you the best way to penetrate your market.

4 Tips for Reaching Prospects with Advertising Media

1. Track your numbers.

According to the marketing viewpoint, you ought to adjust the "cash at a markdown" outlook. We should consider it along these lines...

You're really purchasing clients. Furthermore, you ought to get them at a lower cost, so when they purchase from you, you can procure a benefit.

What amount could you pay for a $10,000 or $100,000 prospect? It's difficult to concoct a figure until you begin following your measurements. Regardless of what promoting media you use, here are the key measurements that you ought to follow:

> **Drives:** What number of leads do you have?
> **Transformation Rate**: In view of the quantity of leads you have, what number is chosen to purchase from you?
> **Cost of Client Obtaining:** What amount did you spend for procuring a client or customer?
> **Exchange Worth (front-end):** This is determined by partitioning the all out worth of all deals by the absolute number of deals.
> **Lifetime Worth (back-end):** This is the typical measure of cash your clients will spend on your business over the whole range of your relationship.

The initial two key measurements are straightforward. Be that as it may, do you have any idea what front-end and back-end mean?

> **Front-end:** This could be a client's most memorable buy from your promotion.
> **Back-end:** This is how much cash you gain from ensuing buys. You either have a membership or a continuous sort of administration.

The objective is to bring in cash on both the front-and back-end. It's to be expected to lose cash toward the front, and procure from the back-end, however in a perfect world you need a profit from venture forthright.

Over the long haul, your numbers will change. They'll go up or down. A slight expansion in each number has a colossal effect on the general outcomes you will get. That is the reason it's vital you know your numbers. Try not to depend on gauges since they're simply a mystery.

However long you track your key measurements consistently, you'll realize the amount you're acquiring and losing. What's more, above all, this will assist you with sorting out the right media stages that turn out best for your business.

2. Don't be single-source dependent.

So, being a single-source dependent is an extremely hazardous methodology in promoting. Try not to be that individual who's getting every one of their leads from one spot, whether it be Google, Facebook, or Amazon. All you want is for one individual to grumble and you can lose your Facebook account overnight. All of your devotees — gone. You'll have absolutely no chance of reaching them.
While a solitary stage can be excellent for you, broadening your media is as yet significant.

I for one suggest you use something like five distinct media stages to assemble associations, promote in, get drives from, and gain income from. For instance, media pitching is an incredible method for acquiring free press for your business and producing leads.

For promoting beginners, you need to have a blend of computerized media and disconnected media. They're truly not excessively confused. Here, I'll unload them for you.

3. Digital Media

You can assemble your pick in list and develop your client base through computerized media. The fundamental motivation behind why my site exists is to have individuals pick into my mailing list. One of my key computerized resources drives my business development.
There are a lot of better places where somebody can select in, whether it's on the landing page, item page, and, surprisingly, on the blog webpage.

Beside your site, you can likewise utilize:

- ➢ **Social Media Platforms:** Facebook, Instagram, LinkedIn, Twitter, and other
- ➢ **Media sharing stages:** TikTok, YouTube, and Spotify
- ➢ **Shopping and internet business stages**: Amazon, Ebay, AliExpress, Etsy
- ➢ **Advertising:** Contributing substance to distributors through official statements or pitching.

Offline Media

Otherwise called customary channels, it's the way organizations promoted in bygone times. Furthermore, your business can in any case profit from:

➢ Radio
➢ Television
➢ Boards
➢ Post office based mail (snail mail)

Like I said, I don't feel that disconnected media is dead. I for one receive many messages a day, however I could get a couple of bundles conveyed to my home. So on the off chance that you're sending me a bundle through actual mail, it will get a greater amount of consideration since I seldom get one.

Presently, if both computerized and disconnected media works, I believe you should adopt a sight and sound strategy. I'm not saying that you ought to be on each stage you run over, however pick media where you can interface with individuals on a continuous premise.

3. Hire experts.

Your publicizing media is the most costly piece of your showcasing. Why? Since it's the extension among you and your objective market. A typical error individuals make is getting compensated for crowding felines.

Assuming that they need something done well, they're essentially involved to do everything all alone. They arrange the appropriate instruments and assets to appropriately ensure everything's working.

Assuming you're doing likewise, reconsider. Try not to overburden yourself, attempting to make everything work. On the off chance that you're not a specialist in a specific region, employ another person to finish the work for you.

Business is a group activity. So in the event that you don't have the foggiest idea how Facebook Promotions work, recruit a Facebook advertisements master. On the off chance that you're new to email advertising and you're battling to make the ideal email, acquire an email promoting trained professionals, etc.

Like any group activity, you want various abilities inside the group. So this is the thing you ought to do:

➢ List every one of the media stages you might want to use for your showcasing. However, first ensure that your objective market is dynamic on these stages.
➢ Contract experts to update your group.
➢ Acquire your expert house.

4. Utilize various devices.

There is no across the board instrument. Indeed, there are some, yet they're not even close to as modern as expert devices.It could sound amusing, however I truly wish that there was one device that would make our lives more straightforward. I've seen that endeavor to do this, yet the issue is they will quite often be unremarkable at everything.

It's comparable while recruiting a woodworker to fabricate a cabinet or racking for my room. I anticipate that he should carry a tool kit with various types of devices inside. Presently, on the off chance that he accompanies an across the board device, I would address regardless of whether he's an expert.

Same thing applies to the instruments you're utilizing for your media methodology. You really want various apparatuses for group correspondence, taking installments, CRM, etc.

The following are 5 apparatuses I'd suggest:

1.Team Communication
  - ➤ G-Suite
  - ➤ Slack
  - ➤ Zoom

In the event that you're fabricating a virtual business, these devices are an unquestionable requirement. My group utilizes G-Suite for the most part for sending and getting messages, putting together reports, etc. We convey day to day through Slack. Whether you're working with a major or little group, it's a decent correspondence stage. You'll likewise require a different instrument for group gatherings like Zoom,

2. Schedule and Planning
  - ➤ Google Schedule
  - ➤ Calendly
  - ➤ Google Schedule provides your group with an outline of how your timetable looks.

What's more, for Calendly, you can plot dates when you're free and permit individuals to book themselves. What's more, it works across time regions too. Let's assume you have a client in an alternate time region, it naturally changes over the time in view of where you reside, settling on booking decisions is very straightforward — and it truly saved me and my group such countless migraines.

3. CRM Frameworks
  - ➤ Ontraport
  - ➤ ActiveCampaign
  - ➤ ConvertKit

Ontraport's my undisputed top choice. It turns out best for mailing records with in excess of 10,000 supporters. ActiveCampaign and ConvertKit are additionally truly well known CRM frameworks. They're great for more modest records.

On the off chance that you're searching for a framework, contemplate how it can assist you with taking pick ins from your site. Search for a CRM that can fragment, has mechanization capacities, and permits you to save your opportunity to deal with other significant issues.

4. Internet Preparing
➤ Zoom Online courses
➤ GoToWebinar
➤ Vimeo

I run an online course no less than one time each week, and I as of now use Zoom Online courses. It records in HD and has this multitude of extravagant highlights like question and answer sessions and surveying.

You can likewise watch out for GoToWebinar and Vimeo. They're both brilliant. Web based preparing and online courses are such a strong mechanism for changing over leads in the pipe.

5. Installment Channels
➤ ThriveCart
➤ SamCart
➤ Shopify
➤ Magento
➤ WooCommerce

I for one use ThriveCart. There are other contending frameworks like SamCart. Assuming you're an internet business, try Shopify, Magento or WooCommerce.

Anything framework you pick, ensure it coordinates with your CRM framework. For instance, when somebody purchases from you, you ought to have the option to label them as a purchaser, so you're done sending prospect-style messages. It's a waste of time to send showcasing messages on the off chance that somebody has previously purchased from you.

What's more, obviously, you really want a straightforward and clean connection point. Some checkout pages simply make things muddled. Try not to add insignificant fields, direct somebody to make a record, and all of this kind of stuff. Make the installment interaction smooth and consistent for everybody

Summarily there are a ton of ways of arriving at possibilities through the media. Try not to depend on one specific media. It requires investment to attempt new things and check whether they work for your Marketing yet your numbers will offer you the responses. Use it for your potential benefit and concoct an incredible system that converts possibilities to clients.

Media is an essential stage in your promotion plan, so you truly need to take care of business. To look further into how to work out your promotion plan, look at this post.

Chapter 3

Capturing Leads

Marketers make a solid effort to direct people to their site, from Website design enhancement to PPC promotions and virtual entertainment crusades. However, the genuine test starts after guests land on your site when now is the ideal time to catch and change over.

Changing over well deserved traffic isn't only quite possibly the greatest test advertisers face however a first concern.

67% of organizations use lead generated as the sole measurement to decide content achievement.

An urgent piece of building an effective lead age process is catching your leads. This imperative step centers around gathering that terrifically significant contact data and information of your planned purchasers.

Leads are the backbone of each and every business. With an incredible lead catch technique, you can diminish your skip rate and convert your guests into quality leads.

In this lead catch guide, we reveal the accepted procedures and strategies for actually changing over and catching leads on your site.
What does the future hold?

- ➢ What is lead capture?
- ➢ Why ditch traditional lead capture forms?
- ➢ Types of high-converting lead capture tactics
- ➢ How to optimize lead capture
- ➢ How to get started

What is lead capture?

Lead capture is the activity that occurs on your site when your guests convert into leads. Regularly this happens utilizing lead catch structures, lead catch pages, and in web based business on checkout pages.

Lead capture is a method for gathering data about your guests (for example name, telephone number, email address, and so on.). This is so you can reach out to them later on and convert them into paying clients. This information is typically assembled through a lead catch structure.

The two most well known sorts of lead capture structures are **in-page structures and popup structures.**

i) In-page structures are implanted into your standard website page and for the most part have a couple of fields and submit buttons.

ii) With popup structures, the sign-up shows up in a popup, and ordinarily, they show offers to your guests. You can likewise utilize tacky bars, side messages, and committed lead catch pages to develop your leads data set.
Ordinarily, guests enter their contact data into a lead catch structure in return for an advantage of some sort or another. This can either be a markdown code, free digital book, a free online class, or a free preliminary.

A lead capture Form: is an instrument used to gather client information. The fundamental reason for lead catch structures is to gather contact data by giving clients something in return for their information - be it an aide, rebate code, or an item demo.

Lead Capture Pages: are devoted points of arrival utilized for explicit advertising efforts. The focal point of lead catch pages is to give data and tempt guests to leave their information. This data is in many cases gathered through lead catch structures.

Why ditch conventional lead capture Forms?

Albeit the common in-page structures are currently at the core of most lead age methodologies, customers have become progressively requesting, defensive of their information, and avoiding leaving their subtleties.

The truth of the matter is that static forms simply don't function as well as they used to. Long form can barely be known as the best lead generation tools, as they never again offer sufficient benefit for guests. Forms with numerous fields can lessen transformation rate.

Marketers have frequently faced an impasse circumstance, the less fields you use, the better the transformation. However, the more fields you have, the better your lead quality.

The issue with standard static forms is that you need to pick either.

By utilizing strategies that are seriously captivating and intuitive like multistep structures or lead generation chatbots you can gather more information in an easy to use way while expanding the nature of your lead capture. Both B2C and B2B lead generating fall under this.

Types of high-converting lead generation tactics:

In this part, we profound plunge into two unique sorts of lead capture strategies for increased conversion rate and further increased customer engagement.

1) Multi Step forms for lead capture

Multi Step structures are precisely the exact thing they sound like - longform broken into different perspectives. It's a basic method for assisting battle with framing weariness and making forms with different fields less overpowering to guests.

Multi-step forms have 300% more conversion.

Clearly, this doesn't imply that sky's the cutoff - it's as yet essential to be compact and downplay structure fields. In any case, in circumstances when it's totally crucial to have many fields, multi-step forms are an extraordinary decision.

Take transporting forms or occasion enrollment for instance - you would have zero desire to send your items to some unacceptable location. Utilizing multi-step forms permits you to gather more data without over-burdening your forms.

When to utilize multi step forms?

Spreading data across various perspectives can make a more certain client experience and increment transformations while further developing your lead quality.

Pick multi-step structures, when you need to:

- ➢ Get a great deal of data and information to qualify leads.
- ➢ Qualify leads without threatening site guests and without diminishing your transformation rate.
- ➢ Just believe guests who are really inspired by your proposition.

BEST PRACTICE TIP! Continuously request the most pivotal data first i.e email or telephone number. Consider making less significant data discretionary.

Peruse more about enhancing your multi-step structures and planning lead catch structures for openness here.

2) Chatbots for capturing more leads

Lead generation chatbots give another road to capturing leads on your site. Albeit frequently considered a client care channel, chatbots are great devices for showcasing and deals.

The advantage of utilizing chatbots for lead capturing:

- ➤ Further developed client experience
- ➤ Capture leads every minute of every day
- ➤ Lead capability
- ➤ Expanded commitment and cooperation

Qualify your leads with chatbots

Similar to multi-step forms, chatbots can work on the nature of your lead capture. Chatbots can assist you with getting more data on leads before you send them to your outreach group.

The explanation that lead generation chatbots are more compelling than static forms is that the lead capture and capability approach is conversational and less pushy!

Consolidate your chatbot with live talk

Lead generation chatbots can be joined with live talk. Utilizing a chatbot as the underlying collaboration, you can qualify the web-based prospect before the exchange to a genuine talk specialist.

This implies your outreach group invests less energy visiting unimportant leads and additional time on qualified prospective customers.

Right now, there are a few arrangements out there that permit you to effectively make chatbots for lead capture. Take giosg, for instance, a flexible device making multi-step forms and lead generation chatbots simple.

3. Use instinctive item demos for getting leads

For items like programming, consider adding an intuitive walkthrough of your item, which closes with a lead structure. For what reason do this? Since purchasers simply need to see the item, prior to concluding whether they'll converse with deals specialists (or sign up).

Utilizing intuitive item demo programming, you can make a bit by bit visit which shows off your UI and key selling focuses in a considerably more captivating manner than just with screen captures.

On the other hand, you can add QR codes with designated CTA utilizing a QR code generator programming. Adding QR codes to your item demo allows you to land your leads on the designated page absent a lot of issues.

You can expect site change rates to expand since it's significantly more alluring to draw in with an intelligent demo versus a plain structure. Utilizing these additionally eliminates bad quality leads who are only inquisitive to see the item.

Any individual who actually books a demo or joins in the wake of going through the visit will be exceptionally drawn in and more probable qualified.

How to optimize your lead capture?

There are numerous ways you can further develop your lead catch methodologies. We've recorded our main three different ways you can upgrade your current lead generation instruments, whether it's lead generation forms or your marketing chatbot.

Use gamification producing leads

Popular expression or not, gamification is a viable method for advancing your lead capture forms, by expanding commitment and transformations. Assuming that you're unfamiliar with it, gamification is tied in with setting game-like elements, mechanics, or UIs onto your site.

There are numerous approaches to gamify your site, yet it functions admirably for further developing your lead catch structures.

Gamification can assist marketers with making intuitive encounters that make your image stand apart from contenders. Make a significant encounter and proposition esteem by utilizing gamification all through the customer journey to:

➢ Capture new leads and gather contact data
➢ Get more information on existing leads and build up your CRM
➢ Fabricate dependability and encourage better client connections

How does gamification in lead catch work?

Gamification makes a "Stream" perspective, which is the sensation of immortality and happens when an encounter is charming to the point that the individual is totally drenched in the thing they are doing.

Building this sort of involvement for your site guests is a definitive objective, right?

Utilizing intuitive game-like impetuses like focuses, identifications, and prizes, advertisers offer more benefit and increment a guest's inspiration to give their information.

Why not have a go at streamlining your lead capture by:

i) Making tests: Tests function as information assortment focused to portion your customer base for personalization. Influence the force of gamification with a tomfoolery test that enacts clients permitting you to engage guests while capturing leads.

ii) Gamifying your occasional missions: Exploit various occasions to gamify your site lead capture.Take a stab at making a coming schedule for your vacation crusade that rouses guests to leave their data in return for an advancement, new item, or markdown.

iii) Making fun polls: Why not make game-like surveys to get a superior comprehension of your current customers, get more data on your customers and beef up your CRM.

iv) Involving gamification in your promotion lead capture forms: Gamify your advertisements by making tests, surveys, or games and interfacing them to outsider sites as rich media advertisements. Interface with your interest group where they are and begin capturing leads beyond your own site!

Center around your lead get methodologies

On the spot friendly displaying is generally called close by re-advancing and is a data driven framework to alter, interface with and get leads on your site.

It's adequate not to just have different lead get procedures set up, zeroing in on your visitors flawlessly is the key for extended changes. Zeroing in on is connected to redoing your system.

80% of clients will undoubtedly work with an association that offers tweaked experiences.

By following your visitor lead and using that data to partition your clients, you can perform productive on the spot zeroing in on. Moreover, accepting your disregard to zero in on your visitors splendidly, it could hinder you.

78% of clients itemized leaving an association's site and purchasing from a competitor due to a deficiently tweaked understanding.

Whether it's multi-step designs, tests or chatbot ensure that each visitor gets a clever experience that is relevant to them.

Have a go at zeroing in on your lead get procedures according to:

➢ What page your visitor is on

➢ Where your visitors are on your page

➢ Where they came from past page, campaign URL, traffic source

➢ Which country they are from

➢ The times they have been on your site

4. Utilize A/B Testing to improve lead changes

A/B testing, otherwise called split testing, includes showing two unique varieties of your substance to your web-based guests.

The exhibition of the two variants is estimated, then assessed, and used to enhance your satisfaction. The point is to decide, which variety performs better for the given change objective.

Tests are best while testing each particular variable in turn, for example, **CTA**s or

forms fields. This makes it conceivable to reach determinations.

While improving your lead capture strategies, you can AB test specific form elements or even different types of lead capture techniques.

A/B testing is the main favored technique for change streamlining by computerized advertisers.

What is the A/B test?

A/B testing is the most well known enhancement technique among advertisers, however right now, not many instruments offer Stomach muscle testing for chatbots or other intuitive lead catch strategies.

Here are a few thoughts of what you could test:

> ➤ Multi-step forms versus a lead generation chatbot
> ➤ Robotized messages of lead generation chatbots
> ➤ The quantity of required forms fields
> ➤ Calls - To Take actions

- ➤ Focusing on: Figure out which page is your most noteworthy changing over page.
- ➤ Instructions to get everything rolling with Intelligent Lead generation

There are numerous things marketers can do to upgrade site changes. In any case, lead capture forms are one of the easiest and best components that give fast and significant yields.

.

Chapter 4

Nurturing Leads

Effective lead nurturing expects the necessities of the purchaser in light of who they are (utilizing profile qualities, like title, job, industry, etc) and where they are in the purchasing system. Nurturing keeps possibilities connected by giving the most important substance (like specialized briefs, digital books, and online courses) for their circumstance. In the event that they get along nicely, lead nurturing can be major areas of strength for constructing devotion well before a possibility is prepared to purchase.

By developing inert interest, organizations can build the transformation of unfit prompts amazing open doors and drive more income. Nurturing additionally speeds up dynamic open doors by giving imminent purchasers the data they need to go with buying choices. Lead nurturing is tied in with aiding purchasers along in their instructive excursion. Which is the reason it's best when set off by prospect action or ways of behaving.

Lead executives ' advances are frequently used to robotize such ongoing promotion. This kind of programming makes it conceivable to follow leads and robotize content conveyance while at the same time gathering social information and setting off related activities.

Understanding lead nurturing

Few out of every odd possibility is prepared to purchase now. As a matter of fact, as per research firm SiriusDecisions, of the 20% of leads that agents circle back to, 70% are not qualified. However, it's an error to disregard those leads. All things considered, 80% of possibilities that don't measure up today will proceed to purchase from somebody inside the following two years. Also, when they do, you maintain that your organization should be at the highest point of their short rundown.

When possibilities are in the channel, supporting them with accommodating, important substance moves likely purchasers through each phase of thought at a characteristic speed until they're fit to be given to deals. Support is the security net for each phase of the purchasing cycle, guaranteeing that no income opportunity is missed.

Lead nurturing regularly centers around changing over contacts that are as of now scored well inside your advertising data set, not creating new requests. This works on the consequences of leads previously accumulated. Request Gen Report found that sustained leads produce a 20% expansion in deals open doors versus non-supported leads.

Without lead nurturing, requests in your framework are just hand-raisers — they've exhibited interest, yet require further profiling and development before they get passed to deals. Lead Nurturing is the interaction that gets that going.

Lead nurturing basics

Marketers frequently erroneously consider lead nurturing as just email correspondence. All things being equal, you ought to consider lead nurturing as a work process, or series of correspondences, in which each step has a reasonable and compact goal — whether moving somebody to the following stage or driving another positive activity.

Compelling nurturing consolidates questions, which assist you with gathering the data important to ceaselessly refine the significance of your messages and move possibilities through the purchasing cycle. Building enduring connections in view of trust requires broad information on your possibilities. Really at that time might you at any point furnish them with the most pertinent substance, informing, and resources. Nurturing ways ought to be founded on special customer profiles. Coming up next are a portion of the vital components of an effective nurturing process:

Segmenting

Segmentation permits you to utilize title, job, industry, or deals stage to represent subtleties in informing. Along these lines, you can guarantee your content resonates with the recipients and reduce unsubscribes.

This isn't only for possibilities. In any event, while you're welcoming another customer, there are a lot of ways of nurturing the relationship and driving reception. Here, as well, is a chance to portion in light of client jobs. Is the client a "champion," "power client," or "leader support"? With this information, you can pipe clients through onboarding programs custom fitted to their jobs, making the change smooth and consistent.

Give to get

At two places in the purchasing cycle, you have prime chances to accumulate data about a contact: when somebody is new to your association and when somebody chooses to turn into a client (or executes new business with you). During these times, you can build the recurrence and number of contacts.

Client center

Use personalization while conceivable, calling the client by name or referencing the organization name. Give resources applicable to the client's business and guarantee that each correspondence is matched to that purchaser's need by then. Every correspondence ought to be intended to respond to a particular inquiry. In the event that you can't respond to the inquiry "How might this benefit the purchaser?" the informing likely isn't important in your supporting project.

Progressive Profiling

Requiring registration in return for a deal is called gating. Nonetheless, in light of the fact that lead nurturing regularly applies to contacts that as of now exist in your data set, placing structures before each offer is excessive. In any case, there are generally holes in contact records. Moderate profiling — which steadily asks contacts for extra data — can assist you with building a rich, significant dataset on each possibility. With moderate profiling, each time a possibility navigates on a proposition, the framework requests only a couple of snippets of data. For instance, one fruitful sustaining program initially furnishes significant level idea authority with no enlistment prerequisite. Then, at that point, it offers a contextual investigation in return for data. Lastly, it guides possibilities toward a demo which they can access without enlisting.

Five moves toward lead supporting achievement

Before you characterize your lead nurturing program, you want to lay the preparation. In this manner, you'll acquire significant bits of knowledge and amplify income potential.

1) Figure out your purchaser

Possibilities go through stages. You really want to grasp those stages and understand what content resources best apply to each. Interview your clients — as well as those that didn't buy from you — to characterize your ideal client profile and foster purchaser personas. What are your client's trouble spots? What buy process do they follow? For what reason would it be a good idea for them to be keen on your item? Characterize what messages are generally suitable at each phase of the purchasing cycle and who is answerable for conveying every correspondence. Great arrangement among showcasing and deals will continue marking, voice, informing, and experience steady.

2) Pinpoint what inspires your purchasers

Break down your past advertising efforts and decide how they added to income. Take a gander at the level of reactions to crusades and decide the number of leads that traveled through all stages, and the messages and content presented at each stage. As per a December 2015 Ascend2 study, 59% of B2B organizations say that making important substance is their greatest obstruction to lead sustaining achievement.

3) Whiteboard the ideal client experience

Think of a lead supporting design that best mirrors your purchasing interaction, then investigate to see where it very well may be challenging to incorporate. Consider customizing the experience in light of what you are familiar with the planned purchaser. Then change the progression of correspondence in view of that individual's way of behaving and commitment with your substance. Begin in view of the last objective and make a plan. Foster a design that checks out for your business and attempt to expect any barricades to execute and make corrections.

When your arrangement is secured, record it with the goal that you can share it and recollect why you pursued specific choices.

4) Plan your lead nurturing process

Decide the mission objective, message stream, content offers, correspondence channels, and in general rhythm in light of past communications. All of this arranging characterizes the timing in your mechanized program. Make certain to thoroughly consider every single imaginable situation. Assuming the goal is to send six messages and settle on three telephone decisions north of about two months, what occurs on the off chance that you don't get the planned reaction? What happens once somebody lapses from a support program? How would you keep that prospect connected with, and who possesses the relationship?

5) Mechanize correspondences

A mechanized welcome mission is an incredible spot to begin. Set up robotized interchanges to welcome the individuals who enter your data set and begin conveying instructive data. What are the three most significant things you believe that they should be aware of? Furthermore, what more would you like to be aware of?

Lead nurturing best practices

In the event that you're prepared to join the business chiefs and start a lead nurturing program, you can build your odds of coming out on top by taking on a few prescribed procedures.

Begin essentially and center around a particular section of your data set with a straightforward source of inspiration (CTA). Perceive how you perform against your objectives and afterward adapt. Whenever you've done this, you can gradually

add ways in view of purchaser persona or deals stage, and customize content as you realize what endlessly doesn't work.

The way in to this is all an emphasis on steady advances. For instance, a welcome program for new leads can be a basic one-two-three touch program that gives new contacts supportive data about the issues your item or administration settles on, the sorts of organizations you help, and where to track down extra data (for instance, directing them toward your most famous downloads). Since you probably have hardly any familiarity with the contact, keep your interchanges conventional toward the start.

For example, send similar three snippets of data to everybody. Then, as contacts consume your substance and invest energy on your webpage, Most B2B advertisers feel that the utilization of promoting innovation is critical to the progress of their lead sustaining methodologies figure computerized non-verbal communication (online ways of behaving that signal aim to organizations) to customize future correspondences.

Contacts are significantly more liable to share data about themselves during the initial 30 days they're locked in with you. In the event that you would be able, computerize touchpoints and utilize a layered structure — or moderate profiling (a course of gathering prospect data gradually and subtly) — to accumulate data. As contacts connect with and move further along the way, you can change this methodology.

At long last, don't overdesign your interchanges. A straightforward text-based email with a significant mark (maybe the President for the main email and salesman on resulting messages) can be similarly basically as compelling as an extravagant HTML email.

Search for chances to robotize. Recognize a conduct trigger (like gladly received, shopping basket deserting, or contract recharging) and enter contacts into a robotized succession where either an activity or a date stamp sets off the cycle.

Utilizing computerization, you can support by stage. It is not difficult to move possibilities into sustaining ways in view of changes leading the pack stage. Through CRM mix, agents can see where possibilities are in the sustaining venture. Construct and send a movement of messages that leads possibilities from attention to schooling to approval. Contacts in the interest stage ought to be coordinated to a program that heats up leads, and data ought to be gathered with every correspondence to guarantee the importance of future messages.

When possibilities are prepared to assess their choices, they ought to be put in a sustaining program zeroed in on training. As they invest more energy at your site consuming your substance, possibilities ought to be added into an "gas pedal program" intended to move them to the following stage in the purchasing cycle. On the off chance that possibilities haven't cooperated with your organization for quite a while, place them into a re-commitment program that decides if they ought to stay in your data set. Comprehend when individuals enter and leave the program.

Since you're speaking with drivers that are not in the dynamic deals cycle, decide how you'll prohibit them from lead nurturing once they enter the choice stage.

Alternately, on the off chance that they're not prepared to purchase, decide how to once again introduce them to your sustain program. When possibilities are further down the channel, cautiously oversee avoidances. You would rather not send computerized messages that copy your agent endeavors.

Then, you want to quantify adequacy. Whenever you've carried out your nurturing program, screen it for viability by contrasting your objectives with the right

measurements. By characterizing your program's motivation, you'll come to comprehend which key execution markers (KPIs) you want to follow.

The simplest spot to begin is by evaluating commitment, for example, email open and navigate rates. On the off chance that these numbers are low, change your messages, timing, and recurrence until you see improvement. Assuming the objective is to move leads starting with one phase then onto the next, track and measure the number of people taking that leap and how lengthy it takes overall. Assuming the objective is to speed up development through the pipeline, measure the days that it takes to advance through the deals cycle. Reliably break down and consistently change your program to represent changes on the lookout, client conduct, and, surprisingly, your association.

i) Client Nurturing
When deals open doors, convert them to clients, enter them in nurturing programs that form dedication and drive reception.

ii) New client onboarding program

You can probably computerize some part of the onboarding experience to drive consistency and increment reception and utilization of your item or administration.

iii) Product reception program

At the point when a record plunges with regards to identifiable exercises, for example, programming logins, you can enter the client into a low-use sustain program. Those clients are then sent messages posing inquiries like the following:

> ➤ Has anything changed in your association?
> ➤ Has your power client continued on?
> ➤ Do you really want to seriously prepare?

You can then make them mindful of assets to keep up with past action levels.

iv) Contract reestablishment program

Ninety days from contract reestablishment, send an email saying, "Your agreement recharging is coming up. Do you have any inquiries?" At 60 days, send an email saying, "Here's your agent's contact data and insights regarding your restoration." Thirty days out from reestablishment, send an email saying, "We'll reach you soon about your agreement." This program heats up your clients so they aren't astonished when the salesperson calls.

Advance Nurturing Practices

Assuming you're prepared to take your lead nurturing to a higher level, have a go at embracing the following practices:

i) Construct a genuinely coordinated campaign

Tap into the strong mix of human connection and computerization by coordinating email, follow-up calls, and updates set off in your CRM framework.

ii) Consolidate nonexclusive and customized interchanges

Except a few leads are trapped in a specific period of the cycle. For instance, there's been no action for 60 days and no dynamic purchasing an open door — yet you need to keep in contact. Send an email like clockwork, maybe about your administrations or about a specific subject. Mix this correspondence with mechanized messages that imitate the involvement in the agent: "Would you say you are prepared to talk? We'd very much want to work with you on the grounds that … "

iii) Coordinate email and outbound teleprospecting

One medium is rarely sufficient to finalize a negotiation.

iv) Reconnect lost bargains/no choice

In the event that you catch bargains you've lost to the opposition or were precluded during the deals cycle, mechanize an occasional connection correspondence to check in. Check whether these leads stay happy with their merchant or are prepared to reconnect with your organization. For a customized touch, send the email for the salesman that dealt with the relationship.

v) Enable agents

As salesmen add names to your contact information base, enable them to add those names to a sustaining program too. Along these lines, they feel sure that contacts are being heated up in a flash.

Lead scoring next stages

The ideas, best practices, and tools shrouded in this chapter will assist you with starting further developing lead sustaining today. Yet, you actually should be ready for what's to come.

➢ Conveying a tweaked experience through your site or web-based entertainment. Advertisers need to sustain individuals in the channels they like, conveying similar sorts of content and data they'd normally convey by means of robotized messages. These channels incorporate web-based entertainment and the organization's site.

➢ Taking special care of how individuals purchase. Utilizing known data about purchaser conduct, advertisers will begin to anticipate whether various blends or sorts of correspondences will impact reaction.

➢ Affecting the discussion by including more data sources. The more you know, the more applicable your discussion will be. This thus implies you will have a superior possibility changing your possibility completely to the following stage. Going ahead, advertisers will begin amassing experiences from different sources — including CRM, LinkedIn, and promoting computerization frameworks — to hoist the degree of discussion.

➢ Mechanizing the relationship all through the purchasing cycle. As advertisers embrace promoting mechanization, CRM, and granular estimations — and develop more adroit at following purchasing cycle stages — they will turn out to be better ready to focus on the right message to the perfect individual at all phases of the purchasing cycle.

➢ Better coordinating virtual entertainment and request age. Advertisers can compensate individuals for commitment in friendly channels. For instance, B2B advertisers could add possibilities to a celebrity program whenever they've arrived at a specific edge of commitment.

With by far most leads neglecting to switch over completely to deals, organizations can't stand to just forsake possibilities when they neglect to become purchasers inside an assigned time span. Especially in the present purchaser driven commercial center, where they are engaged to pursue informed business choices more rapidly than any other time, advertisers should develop a job in the conversation in a way that is significant to their crowds.

By supporting these leads — or expecting prospect needs and giving them the right data in light of what their identity is and where they are in the purchasing system — advertisers can work on their cycles. By executing a proper technique for lead

sustaining, establishing supporting projects, and following the prescribed procedures illustrated here, you can start receiving the rewards of lead nurturing today.

Chapter 5

Marketing Strategy

Each business needs marketing strategy in any case, making one without any preparation is more difficult than one might expect.

Luckily, you have the ability to develop your association, future-confirm your profession, and become a splendid showcasing planner. You can understand your clients better than they know themselves, see precisely how to make content and send off crusades they love, and come by solid outcomes that power deals. So, you can prevail at market strategy.

A marketing procedure alludes to a business' general strategy for arriving at planned purchasers and transforming them into clients of their items or administrations. A marketing technique contains the organization's incentive, key brand informing, information on track client socioeconomics, and other undeniable level components.

A careful marketing methodology covers the four Ps of showcasing: item, value, spot, and advancement.

Understanding Market Strategy

An unmistakable marketing strategy ought to rotate around the organization's incentive, which conveys to buyers what the organization depends on, how it works, and why it merits their business.

This gives marketing groups a layout that ought to educate their drives across all regarding the organization's items and administrations. For instance, Walmart

(WMT) is well known as a markdown retailer with "regular low costs," whose business tasks and promoting endeavors are established in that idea.1

Marketing Strategies vs. Marketing Plans

The marketing system is framed in the marketing plan — a report that details the particular kinds of marketing exercises that an organization directs and contains schedules for carrying out different advertising drives.

Marketing systems ought to preferably have longer life expectancies than individual marketing plans since they contain incentives and other key components of an organization's image, which by and large hold steady over an extended time. As such,marketing systems cover higher perspective informing, while at the same time advertising plans portray the calculated subtleties of explicit missions.

Advantages of Market Strategy

A definitive objective of a marketing system is to accomplish and impart a practical upper hand over rival organizations by understanding the necessities and needs of its buyers. Whether it's a print promotion configuration, mass customization, or a web-based entertainment crusade, a showcasing resource can be passed judgment on in light of how successfully it imparts an organization's guiding principle recommendation.

Statistical surveying can assist with outlining the viability of a given mission and can assist with distinguishing undiscovered crowds to accomplish primary concern objectives and increment deals.

How to Create a Marketing Strategy

Thinking up a marketing methodology requires a couple of steps. HubSpot, a computerized marketing asset, offers knowledge into how to make your strategy.

7 Moves toward Formulating a Total Marketing System

Recognize your objectives: While deals are a definitive objective for each organization, you ought to have all the more momentary objectives, for example, laying out power, expanding client commitment, or creating leads. These more modest objectives offer quantifiable benchmarks for the advancement of your advertising plan. Consider methodology, the undeniable level philosophy and arranging as how you achieve your objectives.

Recognize your clients: Every product or service has its ideal customer, and you should be aware of who they are and where they congregate. Assuming that you sell power instruments, you'll pick advertising channels where general project workers might see your information. Lay out who your client is and the way in which your item will work on their lives.

Create your message: Now that you know your objectives and who you're pitching to,then it is the right time to show your potential clients how your item or administration will help them and for what reason you're the main organization that can give it.

Define Your Budget: How you display your message might rely on the amount you can manage. Will you be buying advertisements? Expecting a viral second via social media naturally? Conveying public statements to the media to attempt to acquire coverage? Your financial plan will determine what you can stand to do.

Decide your channels: Even the best message needs the suitable setting. A few organizations might track down more worth in making blog entries for their site. Others might make progress with paid advertisements via social media channels. Track down the most suitable scene for your substance.

Measure your Success: To focus on your marketing, you really want to understand where your audience might be coming from. Decide your measurements and how you'll pass judgment on the progress of your marketing endeavors.

Why does my company need a marketing strategy?

A marketing strategy assists an organization with guiding its publicizing dollars to where it will have the most effect. Contrasted and the information from 2018, the relationship among association and progress in advertisers hopped from being very nearly multiple times bound to right multiple times almost certain in 2023

What do the four Ps mean in a Market Strategy?

These are the key factors that are involved with the marketing of a good or services The four Ps are:

- ➢ Product
- ➢ Price
- ➢ Promotion
- ➢ Place

The four Ps can be utilized while arranging another undertaking, assessing a current deal, or attempting to upgrade deals with a main interest group. It likewise can be utilized to test an ongoing promoting methodology on another crowd.

What does a marketing strategy look like?

A marketing strategy will detail the marketing, effort, and advertising efforts to be completed by a firm, including how the organization will quantify the impact of these drives. They will commonly follow the four Ps. The capabilities and parts of a marketing plan incorporate statistical surveying to help valuing choices and new market sections, custom-made informing that objectives certain socioeconomics and geographic regions, and stage determination for product and services advancement — computerized, radio, web, exchange magazines, and the blend of those stages for each mission, and measurements that action the consequences of marketing endeavors and their detailing courses of events.

Are marketing plans and strategies the same thing?

The terms "marketing plan" and "marketing strategy" are frequently utilized conversely on the grounds that a marketing plan is created in light of an overall key structure. Sometimes, the plan and the method could be combined into a single document, particularly for smaller businesses that might only conduct a few major missions per year. The arrangement frames marketing exercises on a month to month, quarterly, or yearly premise, while the marketing strategy frames the general incentive.

Chapter 6

Measuring Marketing Results

Marketing groups face a ton of strain with regards to work execution. Besides the fact that they need to drive income, yet additionally demonstrate it.

Without the right measurements, you will battle to demonstrate your immediate (and circuitous) influence on new leads and deals.

Estimating your advertising execution really can at last permit you to screen achievement and quality income back to your promoting efforts.

We saw that only 23% of marketers are sure they're following the right KPIs so it's obviously an issue numerous marketers are confronting.

All that you do in business, you need to have a measurable ROI. This is especially valid for marketing. As marketing has advanced, so has the ability to track it. And keeping in mind that innovation in marketing is fundamental, you really want to have records and processes behind it.

Listen to me.

You can't make a piece of content, push it out and simply leave it, right? Following and announcing, both on the online and offline, is vital for understanding whether your endeavors are having any effect.

Creating leads, through calls, forms entries and live talk, would one say is one thing, yet how precisely do you follow those leads through the full client venture? Indeed, that is precisely the exact thing we're here to share.

Continue reading to learn:

- ➢ The issue with normal promoting measurements to quantify execution
- ➢ Most ideal ways to quantify your marketing execution
- ➢ How we can assist you with estimating marketing execution
- ➢ How you can further develop your advertising estimation

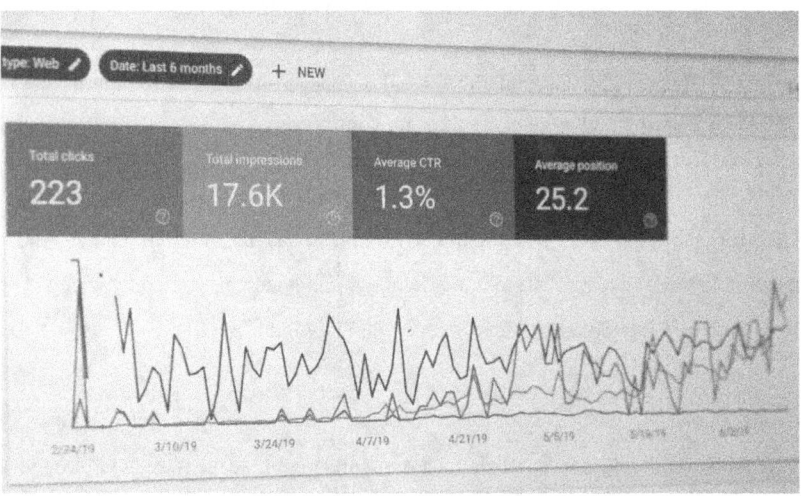

Best ways to measure your marketing performance

Think about the number of marketing channels you routinely use. What's more? ponder on the sheer number of content pieces you discharge every month.

These bits of content are potential marketing touchpoints that a forthcoming client could draw in with.

How would you measure how every one of these channels, missions and content pieces cooperate to create new leads, close deals and drive client loyalty?

To successfully measure your marketing performance you really want to check:

➢ Income and Sales

➢ Lead Generation

➢ Client Retention

➢ Lead Management and Nurture

➢ Brand Awareness

➢ Engagement

Revenue and sales

The primary method for estimating your marketing performance is to closely observe how much income it's created.

Leads

It is possible that you drive leads through your marketing by means of touch point like calls, forms entries or perhaps live talk.

Following every one of these sections is critical to understanding what volume of leads you're passing through marketing.

Yet, there's an issue here. Chances are, you're simply counting the quantity of leads you've produced.While lead volume is significant, you likewise should have the option to demonstrate which channels influence pipeline action. Furthermore, you'll have the option to find out the number of those leads that outs to become sales.

Customer retention and loyalty

Understanding your client retention is mostly for organizations utilizing a membership administration or who need to advance recurrent business. Furthermore, with regards to client dependability, there are a couple of variables in play.

Loyalty could be clients going about as promoters, repeat business, or it very well may be simply engaging with your content.

By understanding how clients are presently interacting, you can more readily recognize what client loyalty resembles for your business.

Lead Nurture

Lead nurture is either overseen by your sales team or passed to marketing automation.

When a lead is created, it'll be pinged over to your CRM where your marketing group will have little inclusion with it.

From that point, your sales group will contact the lead and attempt to advance them through a pipeline.

Once your business is completely enhanced to drive income, you ought to be pursuing accomplishing sales and marketing alignments.

In a perfect world, your sales and marketing groups will be taking a look at the sales cycle comprehensively rather than breaking it into equal parts.

Dealing with your leads permits you to comprehend where in the pipeline they are as of now and steps to take to drive them further down the channel.

Brand awareness measurements contextualize your brand's compass and demonstrate how marketing is growing that awareness. Normal individual measurements that highlight changes in brand awareness incorporate direct traffic or natural traffic for marked terms.

Direct traffic, all things considered, can assist you with finding out about your brand awareness

A few marketers likewise track social media follower counts, the quantity of inbound connections, and the quantity of internet based brand specifications. These are a decent sign of the number of individuals that know about your brand.

Engagement

Engagement measurements range across email, social, online content and that's just the beginning. They basically measure how drawn in your current and potential clients are with your marketing efforts and content.

Common Engagement measurements include:

➢ Social Engagement; quantities of preferences, remarks and so forth

➢ Site Engagement; the quantity of online visits, time on page and so on

➢ Email Engagement; open rate, active visitor clicking percentage and so on

Engagement measurements, by and large, just feature the capability of your marketing.

How we use "connecting the dots" to measure our marketing performance

We've mentioned certain measurements that may appear self-evident. However, it's important to go beyond statistics and give context.

Measuring revenue is more than just reporting on how much money you made last month—it involves connecting each individual transaction to various marketing initiatives, campaigns, and other factors.

Sounds challenging?

We'll demonstrate the process to you from our own marketing team. We employ visitor-level analytics, which enables us to follow customer interactions across the full customer journey, to measure the most critical data for marketers.

or, to put it briefly, Ruler Analytics, our very own marketing attribution tool.It enables our marketing team to examine in-depth the strategies that are generating inbound income.

All we do is link our marketing data to our CRM. We are able to follow up with leads that initially contact us via email and later convert over the phone.

We can also track leads that originate from paid advertising and convert through a different online session in which they fill out a form. Better yet, we'll immediately send it back to the reporting program of your choosing.

You need to observe how prospects and customers are interacting with marketing campaigns and assets, but also with sales teams later on, in order to truly understand the value of your marketing.

This has previously shown to be, at best, challenging and, at worst, unachievable. How come? due to the fact that marketing and sales teams usually operate in different systems.

Tracking metrics like traffic, links, form completions, and time on site are common in marketing. However, measures like revenue, conversions, and repeat/return transactions are often tracked by sales.

Even though measures like links and traffic are crucial, they can only tell you so much about what is effective.

Google Analytics is insufficient for providing a comprehensive picture of marketing performance; instead, you need a platform that combines all of that data.

And since there was no existing answer, we created one. We gauge marketing performance as follows:

1. Monitor anonymous users across many sessions and traffic sources

Our platform lets us track standard metrics like traffic, referrals, and form completions, and we use it to keep an eye on all of our marketing campaigns.

We are also able to pinpoint activities down to individual prospects because Ruler Analytics tracks this data at the visitor level, both known and anonymous.

2. Provide CRM with conversion statistics.

We provide the conversion data to our CRM whenever a visitor converts by phone or form filling. Although we have connectors that can accomplish this, Ruler Analytics marketing data can be sent to over 1,000 tools via Zapier. This adds all marketing data to the sales team's system, enabling our salespeople to better understand prospects' interests before contacting them.

3. Return sales proceeds to Ruler Analytics.

The Ruler Analytics dashboard receives data from sales teams who convert marketing-generated leads and input sales amounts into our CRM.

This provides us with a comprehensive picture of the number of conversions we are making and the precise amount of money those conversions generated. The precise amount of money that various campaigns and channels bring in is visible.

The wonderful thing about reports such as this one is that optimization is made simple.

Suppose you fill out a report at the end of the month detailing the amount of money you made and the marketing touchpoints prospects engaged with before converting.

It's possible that 90% of your income originates from clients who found you via natural search results after visiting the blog posts you've written.

However, just 10% of your revenue comes from your social media marketing efforts, even though you receive a lot more visitors from social media than from organic search.

You can notice that your social media initiatives are not operating up to par because you can now monitor revenue.

On the other hand, your content marketing efforts would appear to be outperforming your social media operations if all you could see were traffic referrals.

However, you now see that is untrue.

The following month, the money earned by marketing doubles as a result of your decision to intensify your content marketing and decrease your social media marketing.

4. Construct interfaces with other web apps

Ruler Analytics facilitates integrations with over a thousand tools and applications, as was previously noted.

In other words, you may access and view all of the data from your Ruler Analytics account by connecting it to your CRM, social media monitoring, and Google Analytics accounts.

For instance, all sales that are linked to a Ruler Analytics dynamic number are delivered into Google Analytics, as you can see below.

Thus, the marketing team can see not just how many calls a source has brought in, but also how much money the company has made from it.

You may, in essence, close the circle between physical sales and online marketing by linking actual income levels and real values to the marketing campaigns, sources, or keywords that produced them.

Final Reflections

It's critical to think creatively when choosing which metrics are important and which datasets can support those measures if you want to assess the impact of your marketing. That being said, it's frequently easier said than done. According to research, 72% of marketers are having trouble locating the resources needed to develop a unified marketing strategy, while 70% of marketers wish to increase their current data capabilities.

Marketers require a performance measurement solution that can compile and evaluate all of this data in one location before they can examine data, metrics, and KPIs holistically. In a world where change is the only constant and a cookie-free future is all but likely, the response needs to be flexible. Teams must be prepared to modify their measuring tactics on short notice.

It will be much simpler for marketers to engage with customers and increase return on investment once they have the tools, know-how, and motivation needed to choose the most significant KPIs.